Drenched
by the Sun

Syam Sudhakar

Foreword
K. Satchidanandan

Sydney School of Arts & Humanities

Drenched by the Sun
Syam Sudhakar

Revised edition January 2016 published by Sydney
School of Arts & Humanities
15-17 Argyle Place, Millers Point, NSW 2000, Australia
www.ssoa.com.au
ISBN: 978-0-9944199-6-5

Poems
Copyright © Syam Sudhakar 2015

Cover picture: Arun Bose
Cover design: Ferdinando Manzo

Previous editions:
Second Edition July 2015
First (Print) Edition November 2013
New Century Book House Pvt. Ltd,
Ambattur, Chennai - 600 0983

Dedication

To
Liz

Acknowledgements

'Thank You' to Dr. P. Rajani, Dr. C.V. Williams, Yuma Vasuki, T.P. Rajeevan, C.S. Biju, Revathy, Raphael, Jemima, Jijo, Kannan, Liz, D. Sreedevi, N.S. Sreedevi, and all who drank with me from the cup of poetry and friendship.

Author Biography

Syam Sudhakar is an award-winning poet who writes in English and Malayalam.

Born in 1983 at Vadanamkurussi, a village in Kerala, India, he was educated in Thrissur and Chennai. Syam has been widely published, has performed readings at home and abroad, and has won a number of awards. His poems have been translated into Tamil, Hindi, Bengali, Manipuri, French and Danish. He has five collections to his credit, *Earpam* (*Damp*) and *Avasanathe Kollimeen* (*The Last Meteor*) in Malayalam, *Drenched by the Sun* in English, *Slicing the Moon* (a bilingual video) and *Syam Sudhakar Kavithaikal* (*Poems of Syam Sudhakar*) in Tamil, translated by Yuma Vasuki.

After completing his Doctorate in English Literature at the University of Madras, Syam is currently based in Kerala, teaching and researching South Indian poetry.

Contents

Foreword
Of fables and dreams

Syam Sudhakar's world is one of fabulous animals, surreal images and omnipresent death. He has an eye for the strange and the uncanny and a way of building translucent metaphors. At times his poems tend to be dialogues as happens in 'Green Sun' or 'Due'. In the former, it is a conversation between the Spanish red and the Indian green - the red possibly standing for the bloodshed in the bull fight, the bullfighter's red scarf, or the red in some of the Picasso paintings, and the green representing regeneration, metamorphosis, like that of lips turning green with the touch of Malayalam. In 'Due', it is Gandhi who writes a letter to Jesus Christ asking him to get down from the cross, leave the church and walk among men without fear as he has already atoned for his sins. But Christ is scared as he is unarmed while Gandhi has a staff to defend himself, besides a cool head. However, the letter from one era does not reach the other as the postman steals the stamps.

Most of Syam's poems have a dream-like quality. In 'Water and Earth', water turns into a sculptor sculpting letters on the strands of rain, or carving butterflies out of fire. In 'Enchantress atop the Potted Palm', the *yakshi* (demoness) of the legends descends from the palm; the poem recreates from memory a bygone age with its beliefs and fantasies. This happens also in a poem like 'From the Mire', where a dead grandfather, a landlord, comes up from the mire carrying a whole dried-up paddy field, clasping a woman's hands. 'I wait', too, has a strong element of fantasy as it presents an elusive enemy who refuses to appear in the candle light of the waiting foe. In 'Digging', the act of digging for a corpse suddenly gets charged with erotic energy turning it into a sort of love-making rite; only in the end the diggers tempted by the woman's inviting organs are disappointed to discover a eunuch's body. The poem in a way de-sexualizes the eunuch too. 'Happiness and Sorrow: A Crisis' is also like a fable or a parable from the Bible where the soul gets caught between heaven and hell. Syam is seldom philosophical, but this poem, like some others, does reveal a philosophical inclination. 'Wax' is another example where melting signifies the evanescence of life and things. In 'The Tea Cup', a man realizes like Omar Khayyam: "The cup and I, [are] both of the same clay."

Syam's world constantly de-familiarizes the familiar as when an ant drops a sugar crystal after a losing battle with a closed window and a man opening the window wonders who had dropped sugar there ('Once an Ant'). Animals and insects – there are poems on a black cat and a lady-spider – fill these fables. In the 'Annual Meeting', we find dogs and wolves, cats and rats, rabbits and tortoises, crocodiles and crickets, bats and owls, though at the end only the ants remain, like a reminder about the brevity of this festival of life. The poet's metaphors have a strangeness about them: 'Barbecuing weariness on the iron-grill of luxury' ('Hunger'), 'waiting for prey listening to the hooves' sounds, smearing poison on grass' ('Trap'). It is a world of flying men, cotton chairs, cheese-cakes for stepping stones and obese lemons ('In the Orchard'); where children are suddenly discovered to be vampires ('Two Little Ones'); where the corpse impatiently waits in the dampness of the mortuary somehow to get dissolved and vanish (Dampness); where Noah sails in an upturned umbrella along the deluge ('Brown Water'); stars are sliding from the sky under the weight of birds ('Below the Sun, Above the Sea'); and a sinking boatman plucks out a rainbow from the sky to turn it into an escape-boat ('The Prayer'). Other poems like 'No one Came' and 'This is What Happened between Me and that Electricity Pole' also have this element of magic in them.

At times Syam's poems tend to be pithy, like haikus. 'The Trap', 'Circles' and 'Waiting' are examples. There are also occasions when his poetry gains a rare musicality as in the lines, "when drenched in rain / he looked like a train" ('From the Mire') or "rheum in the sky / and the fisherman's eye" ('Clouds').

I happily invite the critical reader to this fairy world where childhood memories turn into surreal images and animals, and trees share with man a common world of amusement and pain.

K. SATCHIDANANDAN
Delhi, May 2012

Green Sun

Once an old bird-watcher told me
of the songs of Spanish birds.
Apart from this
I know little of that land.
Huge bulls, ancient churches,
great wars and wooden warring ships.
Nothing to interest me.

I, who prophesy
by reading the stars and the wind,
now think of that country.

And of you seated on a bench
in an unknown park.

Over the phone you ask me the time;
through you, I hear that place.
Without your knowledge, the wind creeps
into your phone reaching my village.

I mark the time of the sun with the sap
of a green leaf from the western ghats,
so that you can read it.

May your lips
that resemble the setting sun of Spain
be reborn green
from a touch of Dravidian language.

Due

Gandhi's statue
posted a five-rupee cover
to Jesus' statue:
'If you have atoned
for all sins
by bearing the Cross
don't wither in the sun
between two thieves.
Leave the churches
and come here;
my people will protect you.'

Jesus replied:
'The sun is not a problem for you
because of your cool head;
rioters won't attack you because you carry a stick.
You are secure
I'm unarmed.
If I come out
your people will attack me.'

The postman
who stole stamps off letters
franked 'Insufficient Postage'
on the correspondence between
two eras.

Water and Earth

she wishes ...
to carve a sculpture from stone and wood

in the rain she carves letters,
under the full moon she carves the dance of
tripurasundari,
into rivers, clouds and waterfalls she carves purity,
light, simplicity,
within the ocean she carves movements

from each ray of the sun she carves a man
and into each of his eyes the pulse of the sun,
drawing the blueprints on the leaves of palms and the
sands of streams

she carves the ages in memories
in fire she carves butterflies;
still the city edges on madness
and hunger hides on the other side of night;
she carves depth in the figureless,
food in the figured,
and the cry of a child in the heart

now she wishes ...
to carve a ship from stone and wood

a sailor with unshadowed face
arises from the ship,

long arms bearing the sun, he swims
over sunken sculptures
through mighty waves
seeking his sculptor

with his fingers in hers
she draws a new orbit for the moon

Enchantress atop the potted palm

"When you hear of Leela, do not mistake me; let me tell you, she is my sister."

M.T. Vasudevan Nair in *Ninte Ormakku*

One such enchanted night
I woke up to discover
you and me
a hill apart

cannot touch
cannot speak
cannot eat
cannot sleep together

a bath together ... never.

'Why so?' I asked
(as you sat over Dad's Ceylon trunk
like a doll)
just as someone
pointing to a sixty-four storeyed tower
rising into the sky asked,
'Wouldn't all die
if a plane crashed into it?'

Like sluiced virgin waters
your dilated eyes
gazing into infinity,
fixed on the vast expanses,
dreamt of a dusk full of wings;
a mermaid, though denying,
counted my wanderings,
gathered my tears.

After marriage

in the quiet of night
you would call,
'Is it raining,
has the mango tree flowered,
how are Chinnu and her little ones?
I forgot the name of the dumb valet
who drowned in the well.
Our writing table in the corridor
give it to me
if not in use.
I know not what I feel ...'

How Alikutty of Vadakketh house
resigned from the Panchayat
due to a quarrel with Dad,
how Regina once cried
on and on,
how we managed
with a single pair of slippers,
how I wept at her marriage
I, who did not shed even a tear
when our father died ...

The spark of inebriate words
creeps up the spine
slowly
transparently.

One such enchanted day after she died
Amma planted a palm in a pot.
'It will only be up to her waist.'
For Amma, she was even now the scale.

At night
as I stepped out,
a girl, just a finger long,
on the rim of the pot,
stretched out her hand to me

for wet lime,
hair spread out,
blue light scattering.

In the heavy fragrance
of the bridal chamber
atop the palm
is heard a brittle laughter.

* *There is a popular myth in Kerala of a Yakshi, a demoness, who, with her enchanting beauty, seduces young men (mostly from the elite class). Asking for wet lime, she takes them to her home on the top of a palm tree and sucks their blood. Her beauty comes from long flowing hair, captivating eyes, alluring smile and the fragrance of pala flower.*

I Wait

At this moment of utmost purity
I await him
beside a lighted candle

something moves
I know him
better than anyone else

the only thing I'm sure of
he is past saving.

Just two seconds more
and then
his veins will writhe on the floor
like a lizard's tail

one moment has just gone by
what remains
is the time
it would take to kill a butterfly.

He has come
behind my chair he stands
trying to talk to me

his breath disturbs me
the dagger handle is crushed
under my tightening grip

unable to endure it any longer
I spring up and turn.

'Who will light a candle at noon?'
he asks and blows it out

and then

like a sudden sound dying out,
he dissolves into the air

for over a year now
I've been trying to kill him.

Tomorrow
at the same time,
beside a lighted candle
I'll wait.

Kaaladeepakam

Here goes the procession of death
through the ribs of dry leaves.

Quietly yawned
the sleeping heart of the peacock.

The blue-neck of writhing death.
Snakeskin entangled the legs.

A rusty Vel.

** Kaaladepakam is an ancient Indian text of astrology.
Vel is the spear-like weapon held by Muruka, the lord
of astrology. He rides on a peacock.*

Digging

the top soil is gone
the colour and texture changed

flowing hair
coloured lips
red tits peeping through the fingers
legs
cheeks
thighs
navel
all floating in joy

the soil may slip

heaving breasts
moist with sweat
tasting of sour lemon
the fragrance of tender coconut
and invigorating toddy
the spades quicken
hitting rock

though blasted many times
the barren eyes of a eunuch
stand out

collecting their wages
the diggers go away

The Prayer

deliberately forgetting to return,
the sinking boatman
plucked a rainbow,
put it in the water face up
and pleaded for an oar
from the anonymous captain
of the wrecked ship

Once an ant

a hand hastens
to secure the window bolt
an ant stares
at the impending obstacle
hesitates
and retracts

holding fast
to a crystal of sugar
it struggles
and squirms
as the bolt careers in

without letting go courage or crystal
it inspects the crannies and crevices
of the dark tunnel

seeking for what it knows is not there

the space shrinks
pressure builds
temperature swings
the heart takes fright

tenaciously clinging to the crystal
it pushes the bolt with its hind legs
it tries
and tries
...

the rain changes its course
someone opens the window

friend,
was it you who carelessly dropped
the sugar there?

From the mire

I dream
a man climbs the back steps
of my house
carrying death on his shoulders.

The rusty smell and the sound
of the cast leg.

Never before
heard of in history.

The swaying paddy field,
its tranquility,
the narrow ridges of the field,
its own crabs,
the same fishes,
the same dream,
the same continuity.

They say that
my grandfather, a landlord,
shifted a whole field
in a single night;
It was before 1957.
No history
ever heard of it.

When drenched in rain
he looked like a train.
Someone is climbing the steps
bearing a field
that withered before the harvest.
Water splashes
into the iron rhythm
of his lost leg.

The field
came to the husk floor
clinging to the grain,
and to the house
clasping a woman's hand.

Identity

Read Nicanor Parra?
Interesting fellow.
Yesterday, a bird
read me poems.
I too feel like
writing a poem.
Why not?
Thus goes my poem:

I
They elected me pimp.
I'm the most secretive
man in the world.

II
Without me
everything will go wrong.
I can die in peace.

III
My birds get angry
when they hear I am writing.
My Lord,
me, a poet! ...

IV
Tomorrow, the first thing I'll do
is to hurl obscenities
at those who don't approve of me.

V
Birdclub, writer's club,
blackness, same race,
I will change my address
to be aware of my own identity.

VI
Praises are showered upon me.
Newspapers flash my picture on the front page.
It's of young Ananda.

VII
I longed to be a pimp
even as a boy.
Why should you be surprised?
I laboured like a dog
to get this status.

VIII
My Holy Vasavadatha,
forgive me ...
For a moment
I forgot
even to remember you.

Shooting star

Short messages on the mobile
friends aplenty –
'Pry fr me
I jst gt my medicl report
conditn s vry critical
as dys pas by I'm becomin
Smart
Cute &
Stylish! ...
Its incurable'

I like girls
and those who engage them.
I also do so,
like '16cm', say, when the sales girl
asks the size

I grabbed her
kissed her, she felt like cotton
got her cell no,
she said, 'leave me, someone will come,'
my shirt wrinkled

I grabbed my bike,
leaving behind friends,
riding wild,
howling,
faster and faster
in the citric-fragrance of the dance bar,
in the dim light,
welling the currency in the beer,
(why aren't these damp currencies as colourful as my
land?)
threw them one by one
some danced for me,
their breasts flying

I checked them,
'the second one is good',
I dined and joked with her

got out for fresh air,
with eyes I sipped
the red sail on the water,
blew the rubber up,
gave it to the girl drying fish,
while going for an ice-cream
saw another girl's happiness
peeping at us, took her too,
went to the cemetery, talked a lot

bye'd and returned home,
bathed, put on kohl,
dressed respectably,
entered the dining room

'girls should be modest'
looking at the clock and dad's photo
mom is serving me rebukes.

Annual meeting

Wild Dogs were
the lords of howl
that day.

Cat led the inaugurator, Rat,
to the dais.
prayer by Hens,
suddenly the electricity went out.

Wolves held aloft
overflowing flames.
voice of the Striped
intoxicated the Spotted.

Frog, the pickpocket
paddled into darkness.
welcome, felicitation, vote of thanks
done in couplets.

Fox playing on Tortoise-tabla
ignored
Rabbit playing on Crocodile strings.
electricity returned
for the entertainments.

Crickets prepared for dance.

Owls tightened the death beat.

Bats applauded feverishly
from the audience.
curtain was brought down,
light and sound were wrapped up.
All left.
As always the Ants
remained.

Hunger

when all is damp
it's not easy to write about humid rooms
perhaps I can tell of those
who live in the haystack

lying, sitting,
barbecuing weariness
on the iron grill of luxury
till a whole rainy season
flows away

the smell of powdery hay
dissolving into the dampness
i am reminded of
toys that scatter
from the dreams of infants
startled out of sleep

and old men exiled
their thoughts
in search of heaven
with cobwebs looking like
the wings of white birds

there they don't have hunger
nor light
not even the wish for a female scent

they see only luminous worms
turning over leaves of languor
one by one
crawling
with little joyous feet
towards the slender calves
of sleeping angelic widows
to stick to them

by their thousand kisses
the widowed skirts dance up
like a calendar in the breeze

The Trap

Listening for silent steps
of hooves softer than snow,
smearing poison on grass-blades
I wait.

Circles

a black circle
in the plain

fear stricken

waves
may come
any time

The Meeting

They entered
leaving politics outside the door.
They must have seen it
'Politics Prohibited'.
I could recognize the fellow with Lenin
only at tea time.

Lenin said:
He's diabetic,
cannot taste love.
Give it to
an ant or a cat
or a breastless female,
whichever comes first.

He sat there, eyes downcast.

I asked: Why lament for
burnt houses and torn letters?
You represent a summer.
It's easy to locate you on maps
from amoeba to America.
To be frank, your views on prose
are an epic unmarred by holes.

Getting up to spit the betel out,
he faced us to ask:
Have you seen my Political Strategy?

Clouds

gleaming crows
weave their nests
in the air
below the pleats of palm

a falling feather
hit by the whistle
of a fisherman
floats up again

a thousand and one wings
doomed for a whole lifetime
send feathers sliding
far above the fisherman

rheum in the sky
and in the fisherman's eye

No one came

Came back to the room
after dinner
forgetting that the key
was in my pocket
knocked on the door.

ΔΣΩ⊤¥

The fellow next door
came out
checked
and without a single word
shut the door.

I put my hand in my pocket
took out my key and entered the room
sat on the cot
covered my face
and screamed.

¥⊤ΩΣΔ

In the orchard

in the orchard
between hell and heaven
a lame young blonde man
flies
carrying a half pound bird.

giant trees
with leaves burning and melting,
eagles chewing their prey,
a bear that shrinks into a rabbit skin
when the wind rustles up snowflakes.

a lizard's writhing tail
quarrels with the body.

a house blown up
beside a river
on the bank of a road

sitting on a cotton chair
with cheese cakes as stepping stones
bent over a woven cane table
a luscious body
full of sweet juice

an obese lemon.

Jagged glass

unexpected

it can happen
anywhere

coarse edges blaze
do it quickly

an initial *ah*
then crippled

the glass wedge
pretends innocence

first a wound
then dry pus
again back to its old state

once the caring become careless
the very mark
has vanished.

Wax

a candle
fixed on the verandah
blown out
frozen stiff in the snow

no one should unfold
the sleep of the bookworm

who is it
that left just two legs
when of a sudden
everything melted down
while wrapping a dhoti around

everything in a moment
vanished
head before a laugh
heart before a tremble
waist before a quiver

on the floor
a melted palette
of black red and white

what remains
two stumps below the knees

go!
go and hide somewhere
before that too melts away

Brown Water

water rises in the street –
when it reaches the third floor
I'll dive and swim like an otter
a mouthful of muddy water
spurting from my mouth
as a rainbow

water rises in the street –
friends, soaked, climb up to
electricity wires
some drop dead and sink ...
the walls of the street form a dam
like a glass
caressing joyous waters
to confine them

when will the chosen noah
who left on an upturned umbrella
return?
his daughter with clayey breasts,
his unsatisfied wife
and a buffalo
all drenched in a topless house

cat soaked
cock soaked
crow soaked

the sky descends through
falling walls
rebukes the innocent sparrows
in regional tongue

swimming, diving,
I cut a pathetic figure
before the television cameras

the ancient street itself
paddles fast
to follow the chosen ones
forming a lengthened
tongue of water

in a boat, a demure *champaka* flower
freezes by moonlight

Happiness and Sorrow: A Crisis

I hanged myself –
the soul climbed up the rope
and reached the sky

I saw two doors
blue green
heaven hell

I wanted heaven
which door?
blue? green?

the knot of crisis
tightened again

the sky pushed down
the corpse of my soul

without me
earth has completed
half its rotation

I fell on the other side –
it was day.

Waiting

None
waiting in this railway station
knows of his yesterday -
he waits
for the train
with hope

In the rain

a heavy vehicle moves
from east to west

the smooth rhythm
of a moped gliding
from north to south
forgetting itself in the
rain

without noticing
they kiss and forget everything
an echo flows with
smooth fluttering robes

onto the black surface
blood spurts
petrol soaks the brain
the heart parts with
the moped

shutting its eyes
the heavy vehicle is
still heading west

abandoning all thought
the rider moves off
south of the road

Colours of Black

In that ladies-wear shop
there are many boys
to handle thousands and
thousands of clothes
from morning till evening
folding and unfolding,
interacting with colours
ceaselessly tired.

When the light walks
away with the boys at night,
those colours spring off the clothes
to giggle and dance.

In the sky, rivers flap their wings
and fly away.

Everyone excited
scatters about the room
spits all around
blames each other
sways and dances
hisses and sings.

When exhausted
they each embrace the watchman's old age
and sleep.
He who was removed from all sounds
finds a torch and bible at his side.
A child, walking to school in the morning
with his bag, shoes and umbrella,
is tired
of watching the colours returning to the clothes,
so tells his father.

But his father, busy,

has been scattered into
the innumerable children.

Enclosed a whole night in a glass vessel,
the boy's father is flying up
over the decaying lake
to the children
with his big leather wings.

He wipes off the children
as their eyeballs and lives
bend like a bow.
The rivers of wings are heard flapping
over the clothes.

A light,
a new entertainment,
the colours the children collected in their eyes
are crowding into the shop
along with the light.

Even amid the rush in front of the shop
without straining his ears
the boy can hear
someone playing marbles with two eyes.

School time

The boy in uniform
has been waiting
on the verandah
for a while.

Yet Amma doesn't ask him
to stop fidgeting and go.

The wall clock did not have
to follow the heart's pendulum
for long.

"Wait. I'll wear the uniform and come."

No one heard the sound from inside
except his friend
waiting.

The animal

above the door,
between the portraits of the hunters,
is that your head on the wall?

your spotted neck
has lost its sheen
and your gaze, its kindness.
your marble eyes
no longer admit me.

your maternal affection
frightens me.
caught in a trap,
squeezed dry,
a discoloured animal skin,
a dead face,
the plain wall of a mansion.

Dampness

it was unexpected

someone's timepiece
cried aloud
to drain the fuel
of my sleep

I have only a thin sheet
against the cold

the cotton above my
parched lips is moist

how much longer
before I leave
the freezing mortuary
where my flesh will dissolve away?

Marble Stones

as marble stones
lean against a wall
inside a shop
dreams are kept aside
for sleeps to come

faint colours
spread at the feet
of a man,
forming a map

the earth
a fertile land
diverse shapes
a garden
a huge onion

onion peel fins of fishes
make waves in the sea

the sea sends a breeze
for the man
with his feet on marbles

Man:
a monument of life,
the wheel of the world

This is What Happened
between Me and that Electricity Pole

Yesterday
as I got down from the bus
there I saw a cobbler
beside the electricity pole.

The shoes he stitches
made from cows' hide
seemed to trot.

I waited, where once the merchants
tied their cattle together
before going to the market,
for those I might never see.

The cobbler stole a sly look
at my ruminating shoes.

This morning,
I got into the bus
and saw the ants
stitching him up.

Now I am travelling,
mind at peace,
my head touches the bars above,
my shoes are trotting,
and I search
for those I might never see.

Cat

I am in love
with a black cat
unbridled, hoofed.
Making love with her
I wish to set the highway on fire.

The smell of
someone
who went before me,
someone
who was caught in the darkness.

It's not about who
but from where.

Police caught me twice
for speeding –
once more
and they might even
have cancelled
my licence.

Amidst this
the letters of
my girlfriend
freed of mistakes
only after several drafts.

Yet I hate letters
without mistakes,
written not to cross her.

Though I agreed to it
with a smile
how can I deny
the black cat

that takes me
to my destination?

Lady spider's suicide note

I came to know of it
only this morning.
We spiders cannot have families.

On mating,
you'd grind yourself,
except for your eyes and skin,
merely to quench my thirst.

For our kids and my own health –
even before the web you'd have made
for your own food
had faded away –
I would eject them,
crying and writhing,
to search for their father,
their eight legs
resting on my chest.
Their little teeth
drawing us apart.

Since I do not want anything of that kind,
Let me do this.

For me you should live.
For me you should not become a father.

A Man and the Singing Stones

John is going to the mill
for some firewood.

No sign of rain.
Suddenly
something cold
falls onto his head and neck.
Searching his collar,
a small fish.

Startled, looks about,
all over the ground
little fishes!
They are leaping.
Rubbing against the mill's roof tiles,
they are rolling down.

Without delay, he gathers all,
encloses them in a crossed box,
and reaches the rock
that groans like a bell.
Whispers in its ears,
'It's fish ... alive'.

A silent song
arises from the big rock.

The paws of three animals
fall on the box.

Another paw emerges from the box.
Far away, John is cooking.
He is singing a wordless song.

Two Little Ones

They are friends.
They come together.
They go together.
They wear similar dresses.

They are friends.
They play, bath,
sing, dance,
walk hand in hand.

There isn't a naughty boy
in their company,
to throw stones at them
to make them cry.

They are friends
of the same age.
They fear their elders.
Elders fear them too.
They are friends.

Untamed,
in the solitude of the burial ground,
sharpening their carnivorous canines,
two chubby little vampires.

A hair falls

You shouldn't ask
why we are being separated
shouldn't blame age and liquor too.

Some of us go that way
that's how we are
uprooted, tangled onto a spiky rod
for weeks, maybe months,
sometimes much longer.

We skip and scatter away
on nails,
on rusty pins,
or on a splinter
or a wind.

Sometimes we return
as a nuisance
seldom we melt away into the air –

like irrecoverable souls.

The Tea Cup

Looking into the cup of tea
I could see vaguely
a woman walking.

The pattern on the cup
encircles her
and the hand bag.

As her waves roll and break
against the other side of the cup,
there a man comes after her
in my cup.

Where did she dissolve to?

Anxiously he searched for her,
I did the same,
looking into the cup.

The cup and I
both of the same clay.

Crouching demurely in the cup
she tints my desire
with cardamom vapours.

A black bag
dangles from the handle of the cup,
all the pride of beauty
immersed there.

All the Lucky Ones

Whenever I attempt suicide
somebody disturbs –
the milkmaid calling
the postman climbing the stairs
Janu bursting in to clean
the thief sneaking behind the dark well
the unexpected black-out
the late tedious trains
the ever-ready-to-help room boy
the traffic police calculating the precise future of
speed,
their unending signs.

Envious joy
when I learn of several suicides
from the papers –

a farmer
a school kid
a family
a nation
alone and together
all the lucky ones succeed.
A girl of eighteen does it eighteen times
sages immortalise themselves by free will
but someone interrupts
whenever I try.

Yesterday there was a documentary
on the various reasons for suicides.
I wonder
do the satellites
panting, sniffing,
capture the minute workings of mind
like video reports on
luminous castles

in the great depths of
the ocean
and the snow-man who walks
from the peaks to the clouds
step by step
and disappears.

When millions of secrets fly criss-cross
like waves, invisible,
when machines in their billions
remain hidden to lick them up,
wouldn't there be a place
for the lost souls of my ancestors to hide?

This longing to end myself
is no longer a secret –
everyone knows everything.
Without any secrets
I become transparent.
I wonder am I made of glass?

Today, when the all-shielding palm umbrellas
of the mire
crossing rain, field, river, hill,
have melted in the towns
like the man who metamorphosed in a tale,
I wish from tomorrow
I were a black sea-turtle.

Below the Sun, Above the Sea

From one star to another, a bird flew
in search of a space to build her nest.
One by one she arranged the words.

Under the bird's weight
stars slid from the night sky.
Taking note, the moon entered a tumble of clouds and
closed
the door.

Next morning, the blue sea observed
another sun in the tears of the bird,
so offered her a space beside its glowing flag,
along a stretched dream sailing its way to Nazareth.

Below the sun, above the sea,
connecting alphabets together,
she made her nest.
There she sat,
a tiny spot of elegance.

Through flickering eyelids,
she beheld the beginning of a life
beneath the arch of a whitening sky.

From the same publisher

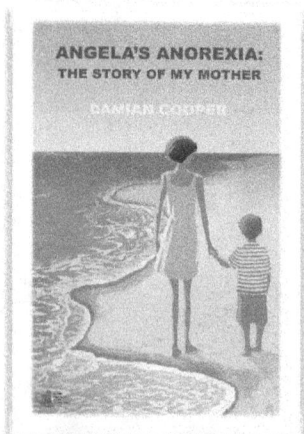

Angela's anorexia: the story of my mother

A son's story of the debilitating illness, anorexia nervosa, that his single mother suffered from throughout his childhood. The mother and son formed a close bond and the boy's description of their life together is filled with both joy and sadness. A true story showing the boy's experience of growing up fast in Australia and New Zealand, caring for his mother while coming to understand her sickness and his need to develop an independent spirit early on.

Damian Cooper has written a straightforward, honest and loving account of his boyhood, set against a poignant parallel story of his mother's excessive focus on body image, food, diet and exercise.

Category: SELF-HELP/EATING DISORDERS AND BODY IMAGE

ARCO:
the legend of the blue vortex

An exciting new story from first-time novelist, Ferdinando Manzo, Arco explores man's battle with the sea in an attempt to seek solace.
The story is set in two different eras: on the high seas among ancient pirates and in contemporary Europe ravaged by war. The legend of the blue vortex – a door into another world – is the central focus of both periods.
An adventure story, it also raises philosophical questions about love and the purpose of life.

Category: FICTION Magical Realism/Romance/Fantasy

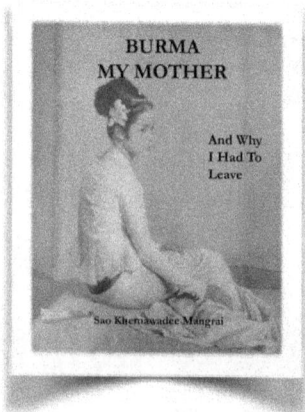

Burma my mother And Why I Had to Leave

Myanmar's future is informed by its past - and BURMA MY MOTHER tells it like it is.

A valuable story of living through good times and plenty of bad in Burma, now known as Myanmar, before an escape to a new life of freedom.

Author **Sao Khemawadee Mangrai**'s husband, Hom, was imprisoned for 5 years, and his father was shot and killed sitting alongside independence leader, General Aung San, when he was assassinated.

Khemawadee grew up in a Shan state in the north-east of Myanmar, previously known as Burma, and now lives in Sydney. Her sad memories are also infused by the beauty of the country and the grace of Myanmar's Buddhist culture.

Category: MEMOIR

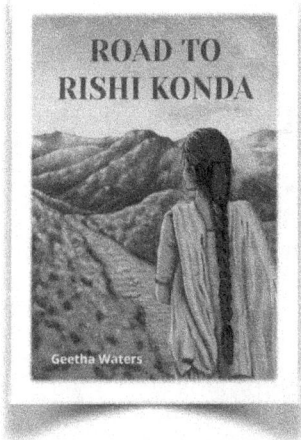

Road to Rishi Konda

'Road to Rishi Konda' by **Geetha Waters** is a memoir of insight and charm, with a serious educational purpose. The author recalls delightful and stimulating stories from her childhood to throw light on the work of the philosopher J. Krishnamurti as a revolutionary 20th century educator.

At once fascinating and enchanting, Geetha Waters' stories centre on a girl growing up in Kerala and Andhra Pradesh in the '60s and '70s.

These youthful tales are underpinned by Geetha's deep understanding of childhood education, based both on her academic studies and in practice in her daily life as a mother and childcare professional. Written from a child's perspective, the tales of awakening to life offer the reader an opportunity to appreciate how all children learn, as they draw on a deep well of curiosity that needs to be respected.

Category: MEMOIR/BURMA-HISTORY

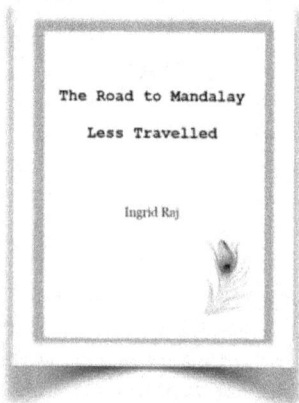

Road to Mandalay Less Travelled

'The Road to Mandalay Less Travelled' by **Ingrid Raj** provides research on a selection of Anglo-Burmese writing published from the period of British rule up in Burma up until 2007. What Raj shares with us in this study is the knowledge she gained about the value of social resistance achieved through writing. Both fiction and non-fiction texts are included in arguing a case that these might be viewed as tools of often ambivalent resistance against oppressive regimes, both local and colonial. Her research deserves a wider readership than was initially provided, and to this aim Sydney School of Arts & Humanities presents the work as its first publication in this new category of Essays & Theses. We hope that specialist researchers as well as members of the general reading public take this opportunity to learn more about the culture of the people of Myanmar through their unique approach to storytelling, based largely on their religious understanding, their rich store of folk legend and their chequered history.

Category: MEMOIR/LITERATURE/BURMA-HISTORY

Jiddu Krishnamurti World Philosopher Revised Edition

The life of the 20th-century philosopher Jiddu Krishnamurti was truly astonishing. As this new updated edition shows, people from all over the world would gather to hear him speak the wisdom of the ages.

Biographer **Christine (CV) Williams** carried out research over a period of four years to write this ebook account of Krishnamurti's life. She studied his major archive of personal correspondence and talks, and interviewed people who knew him intimately.

Krishna was born into poverty in a South Indian village, before being adopted by a wealthy English public figure, Annie Besant. As an adult he settled in California, travelling to India and England every year to give public lectures that inspired spiritual seekers beyond any single religion.

Category: BIOGRAPHY